OWN IT WITH VANAMACE

Van Amace

Published by Van Amace, 2024.

OWN IT WITH VANAMACE

First edition. July 28, 2024.

ISBN: 979-8227382832

Written by Van Amace.

Table of Contents

Introduction.

PICTURE THIS: A COLLEGE dorm room , cluttered with textbooks, assignments, empty pizza boxes with a lot of mess around and a young dreamer which is me off-course . While most of my piers were busy planning their next weekend party. I was on a mission. Armed with nothing but my relentless drive and a stack of property listings, but before diving into this topic let me give you the glimpse into my life before all of this happened that "how this boy who's the notorious, failing and preserved throughout his childhood became the best real estate agent...what is it that happened!!! I know sounds like a mystery right!!!". Here is the spotlight on all of me behind the success scenes, let's first talk about the most excruciating factor behind my personality and mindset development. As born in a very average middle class family doesn't provides you with abundance of choices but my mom never made me think less of myself, doesn't matter how much mess I create in school, or what new weird toy I need this time, she always absorbed it with patience which taught me a whole lot of lessons of which a lot of them I never understood at that age because isn't this a thing in Childhood huh that my parents are not cool enough but I'm so cool they should listen to me every time even if I ask to buy all the toys from store just think about racing all the car together to save this world from all the street dogs ohhh sounds so damn cool isn't it!!everyone will call me hero but who knows remembering that moment from my life sound so silly to me now well talking about being silly, Let's put some light on me being the most stupid that every time I make a fool out of my self my dad just come upfront and just say you are not responsible, you don't understand anything and when will you even grow up. Well he was right and wrong about a lot of things as he was so right about me taking a lot of rush decisions without any solid ground which I accept that made me understand a lot about taking risk and also the importance of planning and risk assessment, well still I was as stubborn as I can be, As I never accepted to anything related to my life on term of others which I always appreciated about myself even though I failed more than 1000 times and had most pubic humiliating moment but I never Gave up on looking forward in my life , I,ve always compared stopping in life as death and movement is life so when I was young obviously I don't have a clue in which direction I'm going in, but always know I want to make something out of myself, doesn't matter if I am born with no generational wealth but I was always dreamt and dedicated to build a legacy of my own. I don't care what I received from my childhood but I promised until I'll be as same age as my grandfather I have to build legacy. At that point of my life it was kinda blurry, sounds like a part from some fantasy land but I was just never been comfortable accepting that this is my fate and I also have to live like the same way my ancestors did, no way in my wildest dreams that was accepted so now I began a journey to discover a lot directions, places, opportunity and people which bring closer to my destiny. From there on I did a lot of mistakes, had a lot of self doubts and learned to carve luck from misfortunes, In this story of mine that all we are going to talk about, so you can look through this mirror as most of the mistakes, failures and success of mine so you can learn anything which resonates with your life and ambitions.

Chapter 1: Dorm Room Dreams.

Picture this:

A college dorm room, cluttered with textbooks, assignments, empty pizza boxes, and a young dreamer—me, of course. While most of my peers were busy planning their next weekend party, I was on a mission. Armed with nothing but my relentless drive and a stack of property listings, I was determined to carve out a path for myself in the world of real estate. But before diving into the whirlwind of my career, let me give you a glimpse into my life before all of this happened. How did this notorious, failing, yet persistent boy become the greatest real estate agent, what was it that happened!!! Sounds like a mystery, right?

The Early Years:

Growing up in a middle-class family doesn't provide you with an abundance of choices, but my mom never made me think less of myself, no matter how much mess I created in school or what new, weird toy I wanted. She absorbed it all with patience, teaching me a whole lot of lessons, most of which I didn't understand at the time. Childhood is funny that way; I thought my parents weren't cool enough, but I was the hero of my own story, thinking I could save the world with a bunch of toys. Reflecting on those moments now, it all sounds so silly.

My dad, on the other hand, was a bit more stern. Every time I made a fool of myself, he'd say, "You're not responsible. You don't understand anything. When will you grow up?" He was right and wrong. I took rash decisions without solid ground, which taught me a lot about risk-taking and planning. Despite his words, I was as stubborn as I could be. I never accepted anything related to my life on others' terms. I failed more than a thousand times and faced some of the most public humiliations, but I never gave up. I always compared stopping in life to death and believed movement was life. Even though I didn't have a clear direction, I always knew I wanted to make something out of myself.

THE COLLEGE YEARS:

When I entered college, I was just an average student. My grades were decent, but nothing extraordinary. However, one thing that set me apart was my eagerness to participate in every activity, competition, and event, even if it made me uncomfortable. This habit played a significant role in shaping who I am today. Each time I stepped out of my comfort zone, I built a little more confidence, resilience, and competitiveness.

Whether it was joining the debate club or volunteering for community service, I threw myself into every opportunity. I remember signing up for a public speaking competition despite my fear of speaking in front of an audience. I stumbled through my speech, but the experience taught me the value of preparation and the importance of facing my fears head-on. Each activity, regardless of the outcome, was a learning experience. This mindset of relentless participation and learning became a cornerstone of my approach to life and business.

During my sophomore year, I discovered my passion for real estate. It started with a part-time job at a local real estate agency. Initially, I was just handling paperwork and doing basic administrative tasks. However, my curiosity and eagerness to learn quickly caught the attention of my boss. She started involving me in client meetings and property viewings. I was fascinated by the world of real estate—the negotiations, the strategies, the satisfaction of finding the perfect property for a client. I knew this was what I wanted to do.

I began immersing myself in real estate literature, attending seminars, and networking with professionals in the field. My dorm room turned into a mini office, with property listings pinned on the walls and real estate books piled on my desk. My roommates thought I was crazy, but I was driven by a vision. I believed that the key to success was to go the extra mile for every client even though at that time it is not even in my budget, whenever I had a conversation with my client, I always try to have as friendly conversation as possible to know what they like and dislike and when I meet them I came up with the most unique ability of mine with a pinch of humor.

First Sale :

I remember my first attempt at selling a property vividly. It was a small apartment that needed a lot of work. I had no experience, but I had passion and a willingness to learn. I spent hours researching, understanding the market, and practicing my pitch. When the time came, I was a bundle of nerves, but I put on a brave face and met the client. The apartment wasn't perfect, but I believed in it. More importantly, I believed in myself. I used every bit of charm I had, and to my surprise, the client decided to go for it. That first sale was a turning point. It wasn't about the commission; it was about the realization that I could do this. I could sell real estate.

"one time I was having a conversation with one of my client where he mentioned that, he wants to go to Paris one day...he want to have dinner on Eiffel Tower with his wife for dinner, So next week on Tuesday when he came to look the penthouse. Where after showing all of it, I told him if you buy this penthouse I will offer you a dinner with the view of Eiffel Tower with your wife" then in a very dramatic way from my suit pocket, I slowly and suspenseful said I have something for you wait and get a Eiffel Tower souvenir out of my pocket saying tadaaa. And he just burst out of lough like a 6-year-old and he said you're weirdly funny. Why did you did that man (with laughing) hahaha...than He said like this, I appreciate you man but I'm not sure yet I'm going to buy this penthouse at that moment I suddenly got total blue I thought I made him lough like that and he is saying he don't want to buy this penthouse now, but then I calmly tried to control that situation by saying "alright" with a very awkward silence then he said I want to buy a home,

I think this is not enough spacious to accommodate my family, I like it but I want you to look for a bigger house. than immediately I got into finding a house for him exactly what he asked for I was looking for it like a crazy menace and when I found it, it was like $4 million surplus of his budget. I've again felt like huh, what should I do now I lost my deadline knowing my rent is on my head coming for me, credit card bills to pay than after all this nervous breakdown, I said man up dude at least ask him about this if he can raise the budget " so I called him and it directly went to voicemail then out of no-where after two hours I got his message says "Hi…I was in a meeting, tell me what happened!! Over text." Than I told him I found an amazing house exactly what you are looking for…he asked "what's the listing price??"

Instantly I typed and send it " $13.7 million than he just again disappeared for the next hour "I was totally sure this time he completely going to ghost me this time, he is never going to buy a house from me" then next day after so many follow up calls and messages he dropped a message saying "I had a conversation with my lawyer he will see the house with you on Friday, he know every detail of what I need"...I said alright share the contact details of him. I'll share the address with him. On Friday I was ready with everything to close this deal with wearing my lucky tie and my favorite suit jacket and then his lawyer met me at the location and he was an exact definition of "poker face" all the time I was showing the house all I hear is "hmm" every time I even tried to slip few of my silly jokes as well and he still is as stoic as before than after showing all of it finally he said something "this is good, this has everything he told me to look for"(in Russian accent) I said then let's call him "he called and said, sir this house have everything you wanted" after call he said he will sign the agreement by today and wired me the money the same day... this is one of my best rollercoaster deal after this I handled every sales for his portfolio.

Subtle art of learning:

As the months went by, I juggled my classes and my burgeoning passion. I'd attend lectures in the morning, meet clients in the afternoon, and study late into the night. It was exhausting, but I loved every minute of it. I learned to manage my time effectively, prioritize tasks, and stay organized. These skills became invaluable as I ventured further into the real estate world.

One of the key lessons I learned during this time was the importance of networking. I started attending local real estate events, mingling with industry professionals, and soaking up knowledge like a sponge. I quickly realized that success in real estate wasn't just about selling properties; it was about building relationships. The people you meet can open doors, provide valuable insights, and help you grow. I made it a point to connect with as many people as possible, from seasoned agents to potential clients. Each interaction was an opportunity to learn and expand my network.

Despite the progress I was making, there were plenty of setbacks. I lost deals, faced rejections, and made mistakes. But each failure was a lesson in disguise. I learned to analyze what went wrong, adjust my strategies, and keep pushing forward. It was during these tough times that I developed resilience and a never-give-up attitude. Every setback fueled my determination to succeed.

My college years were also a period of immense personal growth. Living away from home, managing my finances, and balancing multiple responsibilities taught me the value of independence and self-discipline. I had to grow up fast and learn to handle the pressures of adult life. It wasn't always smooth sailing, but these experiences shaped me into the person I am today.

As I neared the end of my college journey, I started to see the fruits of my labor. My client base was growing, I was gaining recognition, and I felt more confident in my abilities. Graduation was just around the corner, and while my peers were worried about finding jobs, I was already carving out a path in real estate. I knew I had found my calling.

———◉———

CONCLUSION :

Reflecting on those dorm room days, I realize how crucial that period was in laying the foundation for my career. It was a time of dreams, hard work, failures, and triumphs. It taught me that with passion, determination, and the right mindset, you can achieve anything. It was the beginning of an incredible journey that would take me from that cluttered dorm room to the heights of the real estate world.

In the end, those dorm room dreams weren't just about selling properties; they were about believing in myself and my potential. They were about daring to dream big and putting in the work to make those dreams a reality. And as I look back now, I'm grateful for every late night, every failure, and every moment of doubt. Because they all led me to where I am today—a successful real estate professional with a story worth telling.

⎯⎯◉⎯⎯

SUMMARY:

Chapter 1, "Dorm Room Dreams," sets the stage for Van Amace's journey in real estate. Starting as an average college student, my relentless participation in activities outside my comfort zone builds my confidence, resilience, and competitiveness. The discovery of real estate ignites a passion that transforms my dorm room into a mini office.

Balancing academics and real estate, I learn invaluable lessons in time management, networking, and perseverance. Despite setbacks, determination and personal growth lay the foundation for my successful career.

VAN AMACE

This chapter underscores that success begins with relentless drive, self-belief, and the courage to pursue dreams amidst adversity.

Chapter 2: The Art of Hustle.

In the realm of success stories, there's one common thread that binds them all: hustle. It's the unseen force that drives individuals to go beyond the ordinary, to push through barriers, and to create opportunities where none seem to exist. Hustle is not just about hard work; it's about smart work, resilience, and an unyielding spirit. This chapter delves into the art of hustle, exploring how it became the backbone of my journey from a dreamer in a dorm room to a top real estate agent.

DEFINING HUSTLE:

Hustle, in its essence, is about doing whatever it takes to achieve your goals. It's about the relentless pursuit of excellence, where every setback is a setup for a comeback. Hustle is waking up before the sun and burning the midnight oil, not because you have to, but because you want to. It's about seeing every challenge as an opportunity and every failure as a stepping stone. Hustle is not just about working harder; it's about working smarter, finding innovative ways to overcome obstacles and reach new heights.

The Early Days:

In my early days, hustle was my constant companion. The real estate market was competitive, and as a newcomer, I had to prove myself. I started by taking on tasks that others might consider menial. I volunteered for open houses, helped senior agents with their listings, and spent countless hours studying market trends. These experiences were invaluable. They taught me the nuances of the business, helped me build a network, and most importantly, instilled in me the importance of going the extra mile.

One of my first major hustles was organizing a property tour for potential buyers. It wasn't just about showing homes; it was about creating an experience. I arranged transportation, provided refreshments, and even had personalized brochures made for each attendee. It was a huge hit, and I managed to secure several sales from that event. This taught me that success often lies in the details and the effort you put into exceeding expectations.

Learning from the Best:

To master the art of hustle, I sought inspiration from some of the greatest hustlers in history. I read books, attended seminars, and watched countless interviews of successful entrepreneurs and real estate moguls. One common theme stood out: they all had an unwavering belief in their vision and an incredible work ethic. They faced setbacks and failures, but their hustle kept them going. They were constantly learning, adapting, and evolving.

The Role of Resilience:

Hustle is closely intertwined with resilience. The real estate world is filled with rejections, disappointments, and setbacks. Deals fall through, clients back out, and markets fluctuate. It's easy to get discouraged, but true hustlers view these challenges as opportunities to learn and grow. They bounce back stronger, more determined, and more focused.

I remember a particularly tough period when I lost several high-profile deals in a row. It felt like everything was falling apart, and doubt began to creep in. But instead of giving up, I decided to analyze what went wrong. I sought feedback, improved my strategies, and worked even harder. I started attending more networking events, reaching out to potential clients, and honing my negotiation skills. Slowly but surely, things began to turn around. This phase taught me that resilience is not about avoiding failure but about facing it head-on and using it as fuel to drive you forward.

Innovation and Adaptability:

Hustle is not just about doing more; it's about doing things differently. In a constantly evolving market, adaptability is key. I realized early on that to stay ahead, I needed to innovate. I embraced technology, using social media platforms to market properties and connect with clients. I created virtual tours, produced high-quality videos, and leveraged data analytics to understand market trends. These efforts paid off, as I was able to reach a wider audience and provide a more personalized experience to my clients.

Innovation also meant being open to new ideas and continuously learning. I took courses on digital marketing, attended workshops on negotiation tactics, and kept up with industry trends. This commitment to learning allowed me to stay relevant and offer my clients the best possible service.

Building a Strong Network:

Hustle also involves building and nurturing a strong network. In real estate, relationships are everything. I made it a point to connect with fellow agents, potential clients, and industry influencers. I attended industry events, joined professional organizations, and actively participated in online forums. Networking was not just about exchanging business cards; it was about building genuine relationships based on trust and mutual respect.

One of my breakthrough moments came when I partnered with a senior agent on a high-profile listing. This collaboration not only boosted my credibility but also opened doors to new opportunities. It reinforced the idea that success in real estate is a team effort, and having a strong network can make all the difference.

The Power of Persistence:

Persistence is a crucial aspect of hustle. There were times when the going got tough, and it seemed like success was out of reach. But I kept pushing forward, fueled by a vision of what I wanted to achieve. I made countless cold calls, followed up relentlessly with potential leads, and kept refining my pitch. Persistence paid off, as I started closing more deals and gaining recognition in the industry.

One memorable instance was a property that had been on the market for months with no buyers. The owner was frustrated and considering taking it off the market. I saw potential in the property and convinced the owner to give me a chance. I revamped the marketing strategy, hosted several open houses, and reached out to my network. After weeks of hard work, I managed to find a buyer, and the property sold for a great price. This experience underscored the importance of persistence and never giving up, even when the odds seem against you.

Balancing Hustle with Well-being:

While hustle is essential for success, it's equally important to maintain a balance between work and well-being. The initial years of my career were marked by long hours and little rest. I realized that to sustain my hustle, I needed to take care of myself. I started incorporating regular exercise into my routine, adopted a healthier diet, and made time for relaxation and hobbies.

Maintaining a work-life balance allowed me to recharge and stay focused. It also improved my productivity and creativity. I learned that hustle doesn't mean burning out; it means finding a sustainable pace that allows you to keep pushing forward without compromising your health and happiness.

Conclusion:

The art of hustle is a multifaceted journey. It's about hard work, resilience, innovation, networking, and persistence. It's about believing in your vision, continuously learning, and adapting to changing circumstances. Hustle is not just a phase; it's a mindset, a way of life. It's what turns dreams into reality and challenges into opportunities.

In the world of real estate, hustle is the driving force behind every successful deal, every satisfied client, and every milestone achieved. It's what separates the good from the great and the ordinary from the extraordinary. As I reflect on my journey, I realize that hustle has been my greatest asset. It's the reason I wake up with a sense of purpose and go to bed with a sense of accomplishment. It's the reason I've been able to turn my dreams into reality and build a legacy that I'm proud of.

Summary:

Chapter 2, "The Art of Hustle," explores the essential elements that drive success: hard work, resilience, innovation, networking, and persistence. It highlights the importance of a relentless pursuit of goals, learning from failures, and continuously adapting to stay ahead. The chapter underscores that hustle is a mindset, not just about working harder but working smarter and finding balance. Through personal anecdotes and lessons from industry icons, this chapter provides a roadmap for turning dreams into reality and achieving greatness in the competitive world of real estate.

Chapter 3: Charm Over Commission:

Charm Over Commission:
How a chance encounter in a coffee shop led to a lifelong connection, proving that relationships matter more than sales.

I WALKED INTO THE QUAINT little coffee shop, the kind of place that exuded charm with its mismatched furniture and eclectic decor. The smell of freshly ground coffee beans mingled with the sound of soft jazz playing in the background. It was one of those rare quiet moments in my hectic schedule, and I intended to savor it.

As I approached the counter, I noticed a man engrossed in a book. He was sitting by the window, his brow furrowed in concentration. The title of the book caught my eye: "The Art of Selling" by Brian Tracy. As a real estate agent, I had devoured every book on sales and success I could find, including that one. I couldn't resist striking up a conversation.

"Great book," I said, nodding towards the cover as I placed my order.

He looked up, slightly startled, then smiled. "It really is. Are you a fan of Brian Tracy?"

"Absolutely," I replied. "His strategies have been game-changers for my career in real estate."

"Real estate, huh?" He extended his hand. "I'm James, by the way."

"Van amace," I said, shaking his hand. "Nice to meet you."

We chatted for a few minutes about the book and our favorite takeaways from Tracy's work. James was articulate and insightful, and our conversation flowed effortlessly. When my coffee was ready, I found myself reluctant to end our chat.

"Mind if I join you?" I asked.

"Not at all," he said, gesturing to the empty chair across from him.

As we settled in, our conversation shifted from books to life and business. James, it turned out, was a tech entrepreneur with a passion for innovation. His startup was on the verge of launching a new app designed to streamline property management. We discussed everything from market trends to the challenges of entrepreneurship. The more we talked, the more I realized we shared a similar philosophy: success was about more than just closing deals; it was about building relationships.

"People often say you shouldn't judge a book by its cover," James remarked, taking a sip of his coffee. "But I've found that first impressions are incredibly important. They set the tone for everything that follows."

I nodded in agreement. "Absolutely. In real estate, first impressions can make or break a deal. But it's not just about looking the part. It's about genuinely connecting with people."

James smiled. "You know, I can tell you understand that. Most people I meet in business are all about the hard sell, but you seem different."

"Thanks, James," I said, genuinely touched. "I believe that if you focus on the person and not just the transaction, the sales will follow naturally."

Our conversation continued for over an hour. We exchanged contact information, and I left the coffee shop feeling invigorated. Little did I know that this chance meeting would become a pivotal moment in my career.

<hr>

A FEW WEEKS LATER, I received a call from James. He had referred a friend who was looking to buy a property. The friend, Mark, was a high-net-worth individual looking for a luxurious penthouse in the city. When I met Mark, I approached him with the same authenticity and charm I had shown James. I listened carefully to his needs and preferences, offering tailored recommendations rather than pushing for a quick sale.

After several viewings, Mark finally settled on a stunning penthouse with panoramic views of the skyline. It was a significant deal, and the commission was substantial. But more importantly, it reinforced the lesson I had learned from my encounter with James: relationships are the cornerstone of success.

ONE AFTERNOON, ABOUT a month after Mark's purchase, James invited me to a networking event for tech entrepreneurs and investors. The room was filled with influential figures, and I knew this was an incredible opportunity to expand my network.

James introduced me to several key people, each introduction coming with a glowing endorsement of my character and professionalism. As I mingled, I found myself in conversation with a venture capitalist named Lisa. She was intrigued by my approach to real estate and how I integrated technology into my business.

"James speaks very highly of you," Lisa said. "I'm always looking for trustworthy agents to recommend to my clients. How do you manage to stand out in such a competitive field?"

"It's all about first impressions and building genuine connections," I explained. "I focus on understanding my clients' needs and delivering value beyond the transaction."

Lisa nodded thoughtfully. "That's refreshing to hear. Most agents I've dealt with are only interested in closing the deal as quickly as possible."

"There's a saying I love," I said with a grin. "'You can't make a good deal with a bad person.' I aim to be the good person people want to make deals with."

Lisa laughed. "That's a great perspective. I'll definitely keep you in mind for future referrals."

OVER THE NEXT FEW MONTHS, the referrals from James and his network kept coming. Each new client brought new challenges and opportunities, but my approach remained

---

CONSISTENT: FOCUS ON the relationship first. The results were remarkable. My business grew, not just in terms of sales, but in terms of reputation and trust.

One particularly memorable referral was from a client named Emily. She was looking for a property to use as a corporate retreat for her company. She had very specific requirements, and finding the right property was a challenge. But through careful listening and perseverance, I was able to find her the perfect place.

During the closing process, Emily confided in me. "Mr. Van Amace, I have to tell you, I've worked with many agents over the years, but none have been as attentive and genuine as you. James was right about you."

"Thank you, Emily," I said. "It means a lot to hear that. I believe that every client deserves my full attention and effort, regardless of the size of the deal."

As the months went by, my connection with James deepened into a genuine friendship. We often met up to discuss business ideas, share successes, and offer each other advice. His tech startup thrived, and my real estate business flourished. Our collaboration demonstrated that relationships built on mutual respect and trust could lead to extraordinary outcomes.

⬥

ONE DAY, WHILE HAVING lunch with James, he shared some exciting news. " our app has received significant interest from a major investor. We're going to expand internationally, and we'll need real estate experts to help us navigate the new markets."

"That's incredible, James!" I exclaimed. "I'd be honored to assist in any way I can."

⬥

"THERE'S NO ONE ELSE I'd trust more," he said. "Your understanding of the market and your commitment to clients are exactly what we need."

This opportunity was a testament to the power of charm over commission. My initial conversation with James, sparked by a shared interest in a book, had evolved into a professional partnership with far-reaching implications. It wasn't about making a sale; it was about building a relationship.

⬥

REFLECTING ON THIS journey, I realized how often we underestimate the impact of first impressions. That chance encounter in a coffee shop had set the stage for a series of events that transformed my career. It was a reminder that people do judge a book by its cover, but it's what they find inside that keeps them coming back.

I often share this story with new agents, emphasizing the importance of authenticity and connection. "Remember," I tell them, "people want to do business with someone they like and trust. Focus on building relationships, and the commissions will follow."

———⬤———

HUMOR AND HUMILITY have been my companions on this journey. I remember joking with James during one of our coffee shop meetings, "Who knew that a conversation about Brian Tracy could lead to international business ventures?"

James laughed. "It just goes to show, you never know where a good book and a good conversation might lead."

———⬤———

SUMMARY:

This chapter illustrates the profound impact of charm and genuine connections in real estate. A chance encounter in a coffee shop led to a lasting professional relationship that brought numerous referrals and significant business growth. The story emphasizes the importance of first impressions and building trust, proving that relationships are more valuable than any single commission. Through humor and authentic interactions, we can create opportunities and partnerships that extend far beyond the initial sale.

Chapter 4: From Pizza Boxes to Penthouses.

In the chaotic realm of college life, my dorm room was a blend of textbooks, empty pizza boxes, and unfulfilled dreams. Little did anyone know, amid that mess, a future real estate mogul was being shaped. My journey from that cluttered dorm to negotiating deals for luxury penthouses was anything but straightforward. It was a path marked by confusion, determination, and a relentless quest to figure it all out. This chapter unpacks that transformation—how I evolved from a pizza-box-clad student to a real estate professional navigating the heights of luxury listings.

<hr>

THE EARLY DAYS: FINDING My Feet:

When I first entered the real estate world, my knowledge was minimal. I didn't understand how commissions worked, had no grasp of contracts, and was clueless about acquiring listings or finding buyers. It was a steep learning curve, and my initial forays were nothing short of chaotic.

I remember vividly my first listing. It wasn't a glamorous property by any means. It was a small, old house belonging to a retired schoolteacher who had called me out of desperation. This was not a property that would attract the usual high-end clients. Instead, it was one that other brokers avoided. I took the listing, not because it was a golden opportunity but because it was all I had. My inexperience meant I lacked the confidence to turn down any opportunity.

The Learning Curve:

At first, I was overwhelmed. I had no systems in place, no sense of daily discipline, and absolutely no accountability. My approach was scattershot—working at odd hours, missing deadlines, and generally floundering. My mornings were filled with random calls and meetings that rarely led to productive outcomes. It was clear that if I wanted to succeed, I needed to make a drastic change.

In the beginning, the real estate business felt like an inscrutable puzzle. I had to learn everything from scratch, including how to draft contracts, handle client expectations, and manage the intricacies of real estate transactions. The only way I could make sense of it was by immersing myself in every aspect of the job. I studied contracts obsessively, attended workshops, and read every book I could find on real estate and sales strategies.

———⬤———

THE TURNING POINT: Embracing Discipline:

As I sought to gain traction, I realized that the key to success lay in adopting a disciplined approach. I started to structure my day meticulously—mapping out every minute and focusing on enhancing productivity. My schedule became my lifeline. I set specific goals for daily activities, including prospecting, follow-ups, and client meetings. This newfound discipline didn't just improve my productivity; it transformed my entire approach to work.

I also recognized the importance of consistency. I began to treat every small task as a crucial step towards larger goals. Whether it was cold calling, sending emails, or attending networking events, I did everything with a sense of purpose. I made a habit of reviewing my progress daily and adjusting my strategies as needed. This consistent effort began to yield results, as I started to build a reputation for reliability and dedication.

Building a Network: Leveraging Social Media:

Real estate is a people-centric industry, and I quickly learned that networking was essential. I used social media as a tool to engage with industry professionals and potential clients. Platforms like LinkedIn and Instagram became invaluable for connecting with colleagues, joining discussions, and showcasing my growing expertise.

I immersed myself in online communities related to real estate, joining groups and participating in discussions. My active engagement helped me gain respect from industry veterans and opened doors to opportunities that would have otherwise been inaccessible. I used social media to demonstrate my genuine interest in real estate, which gradually built trust and credibility within the community.

Overcoming Challenges: From Crazy Listings to Co-Brokering:

In the early days, the properties I worked with were often unconventional. I found myself dealing with listings that other brokers would turn away—properties with unusual challenges, eccentric sellers, or unique circumstances. Despite these hurdles, I approached each listing with enthusiasm and a willingness to learn.

One memorable listing involved a home owned by a notoriously difficult client who refused to adhere to conventional selling practices. While other brokers avoided this property, I took it on as a learning experience. Working with such challenging clients taught me valuable lessons in negotiation and patience. I quickly learned that successful real estate transactions often require a blend of empathy, problem-solving skills, and creative thinking.

In addition to handling challenging listings, I collaborated with other brokers as a co-broker on several deals. This collaboration allowed me to gain insights from more experienced professionals and build relationships within the industry. Working alongside seasoned brokers provided me with practical knowledge and exposed me to different perspectives on handling various aspects of the business.

The Path to Penthouses: Scaling Up:

As I gained experience and refined my approach, I began to attract higher-end listings. The transition from handling modest properties to luxury penthouses was gradual but rewarding. My reputation as a dedicated and knowledgeable agent helped me secure more prestigious listings.

The process of scaling up involved several key strategies:

1. Leveraging Existing Connections: I reached out to past clients and industry contacts, leveraging my network to gain referrals and recommendations.

2. Enhancing My Brand: I invested in marketing strategies that showcased my expertise in handling high-end properties. This included creating high-quality marketing materials and optimizing my online presence.

---

3. UNDERSTANDING LUXURY Markets: I immersed myself in the luxury real estate market, learning about the unique needs and preferences of high-end clients. This included understanding market trends, property features, and the nuances of luxury transactions.

CONCLUSION:

From my initial days of working with pizza boxes to managing luxury penthouses, the journey has been one of transformation and growth. My story underscores the importance of persistence, discipline, and continuous learning in achieving success in real estate. Each challenge faced and lesson learned contributed to my development as a professional, ultimately leading me to excel in the high-stakes world of luxury real estate.

BY EMBRACING DISCIPLINE, leveraging social media, and collaborating with others, I navigated the complexities of real estate and built a successful career. My journey from pizza boxes to penthouses demonstrates that with dedication and a strategic approach, even the most challenging beginnings can lead to remarkable success.

Chapter 5: Epic Fails and Bigger Wins.

Introduction:

"Epic fails and bigger wins"—sounds like a dramatic tagline, doesn't it? But if you've ever had your confidence shattered, faced public humiliation, and battled self-doubt, you'll understand that this is more than just a chapter title; it's a reflection of a journey. In this chapter, I'm opening the curtain on the times when I stumbled and fell, only to rise stronger, more determined, and more successful. The lessons learned from these failures have shaped my career and taught me that the world doesn't end because of a setback.

VAN AMACE

The Humble Beginnings of a Determined Dreamer:

My journey began with a series of missteps and stumbles that would make anyone question their path. Back in college, I was enthusiastic but green—eager to make my mark in real estate but lacking the experience and finesse. My first attempt at selling a property was nothing short of a disaster. I remember walking into that meeting with a sense of invincibility, only to realize that I was woefully unprepared. The property was overvalued, my presentation was lackluster, and my answers to the client's questions were embarrassingly vague.

Public humiliation is a harsh teacher. I was roasted by my peers and criticized by my mentors. I began to doubt myself. Was this really the career for me? Should I abandon my dreams? The sting of failure was palpable. But, as Brian Tracy often emphasizes, "The only real failure is the failure to try." In those moments of doubt, I realized that the opinions of others did not define my capabilities.

Facing the Shadows of Self-Doubt: The first major public failure I faced was when I presented a pitch to a prominent investor. It was a grand opportunity, and I had prepared meticulously—or so I thought. The investor asked questions that I couldn't answer, and my inexperience was laid bare. The presentation ended with polite but tepid applause, and the investor walked away unimpressed. The experience was a public humiliation that haunted me for months.

Self-doubt crept in like a shadow, clouding my confidence and creativity. Every time I thought about that pitch, I felt a pang of embarrassment. But, as I mulled over my failures, I recalled a critical lesson from "Sell It Like Serhant"—successful people aren't afraid of failure. They embrace it as part of the journey. The key is to acknowledge it, learn from it, and move forward. My failure wasn't the end; it was merely a stepping stone to improvement.

The Turning Point: Embracing the Lessons:

The turning point came when I decided to reframe my failures as opportunities for growth. Instead of dwelling on my shortcomings, I began to analyze what went wrong and how I could improve. I started attending workshops, seeking mentorship, and practicing my pitches relentlessly. The mindset shift from "I hate losing" to "I hate losing more than I love winning" became my driving force.

ONE PARTICULARLY POIGNANT lesson came from a major blunder during a property auction. I mistakenly announced the wrong starting bid, which caused a series of complications and resulted in a botched auction. The embarrassment was overwhelming, and I faced a barrage of criticism from both clients and colleagues.

Yet, this blunder taught me the importance of precision and thoroughness. I became meticulous about every detail, ensuring that such mistakes would not happen again.

The Philosophy of "You Can't Do That:

In the face of adversity, one of the most liberating realizations was understanding that when people said, "You can't do that," they were actually projecting their own limitations onto me. This perspective shift was instrumental in overcoming the mental barriers I had set for myself. It became clear that their skepticism was not a reflection of my abilities but rather their inability to imagine my success.

This realization was reinforced by another quote from Brian Tracy: "You can have anything you want if you are willing to give up the belief that you can't have it." I began to see my failures not as barriers but as challenges to be conquered. My approach to every setback was to confront it head-on, learn from it, and use it as a catalyst for growth.

Bouncing Back: The Path to Bigger Wins:

Success didn't come overnight. It was the result of relentless effort, learning from my failures, and refining my approach. My approach to sales and client interactions evolved significantly. I started incorporating feedback, practicing my presentations, and developing a deeper understanding of the market. Each failure was a lesson in disguise, guiding me toward improvement.

One of the most significant comebacks was securing a major contract with a high-profile client after a series of rejections. I had faced numerous setbacks, but I refused to let them define me. My persistence paid off, and the deal not only restored my confidence but also significantly boosted my career.

The Role of Humor in Overcoming Failure:

Humor played a crucial role in my journey. It allowed me to view my failures through a lighter lens and helped me maintain a positive outlook. I learned to laugh at my mistakes, find humor in the situation, and use it as a tool for resilience.

One memorable incident involved a client meeting where I accidentally mixed up the property details, resulting in a humorous but awkward presentation. Instead of letting it get me down, I used it as an icebreaker, and the client appreciated my ability to stay composed and find humor in the situation. This approach helped build rapport and turned a potentially disastrous meeting into a successful one.

From Blunders to Triumphs: The Final Takeaway:

Looking back, I see each failure as an essential part of my journey. The mistakes and public humiliations were not the end but rather the beginning of a new chapter. They taught me resilience, adaptability, and the importance of continuous improvement.

As Jim Rohn once said, "Don't wish it were easier; wish you were better." My journey through epic fails and bigger wins has made me better, more resilient, and more determined. I've learned that failure is not a setback but a setup for a comeback. Embrace your failures, learn from them, and let them propel you toward greater success.

Summary:

In this chapter, we explored the highs and lows of my journey through failures and successes. From embarrassing public moments to significant setbacks, each failure was a lesson that shaped my approach to real estate. The key takeaways include:

1. Failures as Opportunities: View setbacks as learning opportunities rather than barriers.

2. Self-Doubt to Resilience: Overcome self-doubt by embracing a mindset of continuous improvement.

3. Perspective Shift: Understand that others' skepticism reflects their limitations, not yours.

4. Humor as a Tool: Use humor to maintain a positive outlook and build rapport.

5. Persistence Pays Off: Relentless effort and learning from mistakes lead to greater success.

Embrace your journey with all its ups and downs, and remember that every failure brings you one step closer to your next big win.

Chapter 6: The Million-Dollar Listing.

Introduction:

Picture a crisp autumn morning in New York City, the skyline glowing in the soft morning light. It was on such a day that I found myself staring at my first million-dollar listing, a stunning penthouse that would soon redefine my career. Achieving this milestone wasn't just a financial triumph; it was an entry ticket into a world of opportunities that I had only dreamed of. This chapter delves into the significance of that million-dollar listing, the lessons learned, and the profound impact it had on my journey.

The Million-Dollar Milestone:

Securing a million-dollar listing wasn't just a matter of luck. It was the result of relentless effort, strategic networking, and an unwavering belief in my capabilities. The journey began years earlier, in a college dorm room cluttered with textbooks and empty pizza boxes, where my dreams took root. As I honed my skills, moving from small sales to bigger properties, I knew that a million-dollar listing would be a game-changer. But why is such a milestone so significant?

First and foremost, million-dollar properties attract high-net-worth individuals who often have extensive real estate portfolios. These clients are not just looking for a home; they are seeking investments, status symbols, and exclusive lifestyles. Working with them opens doors to multiple opportunities, not only to sell more high-margin properties but also to establish long-term relationships based on trust and mutual benefit.

Understanding High-Net-Worth Individuals:

Selling to high-net-worth individuals (HNWIs) is a unique experience that demands a deep understanding of their behavior and preferences. Unlike typical buyers, HNWIs rely heavily on trusted brokers to manage their real estate transactions. Their decisions are driven by a blend of logic and emotion, with a significant emphasis on trust, exclusivity, and efficiency.

One of my earliest lessons in dealing with HNWIs came during a property viewing with a renowned tech entrepreneur. As we toured the luxurious penthouse, I quickly realized that my usual sales pitch wouldn't suffice. This client wasn't just interested in the square footage or the number of bedrooms; he wanted to know about the exclusivity of the neighborhood, the privacy it offered, and how quickly I could finalize the deal.

THIS EXPERIENCE TAUGHT me the importance of thinking on my feet.

HNWIs value their time immensely, and any delay or inconvenience can be a deal-breaker. I learned to anticipate their needs, address their concerns promptly, and provide solutions without hesitation. This proactive approach not only facilitated smoother transactions but also strengthened my credibility as a trusted broker.

The Power of Trust:

Building trust with HNWIs is paramount. These clients often have multiple properties and investments, making them highly discerning and cautious. To earn their trust, I focused on transparency, reliability, and personalized service. I ensured that every detail was meticulously handled, from the initial viewing to the final closing.

One memorable instance was with a billionaire investor who was interested in a sprawling estate. During our discussions, he expressed concerns about the property's security features. Recognizing the importance of this issue, I immediately arranged a meeting with a top security consultant and provided a comprehensive security plan tailored to his needs. This swift response not only alleviated his concerns but also demonstrated my commitment to his satisfaction.

Through such experiences, I realized that earning the trust of HNWIs could lead to long-term relationships and repeat business. Satisfied clients would often refer me to their peers, further expanding my network and opening up new opportunities. The ripple effect of a single successful transaction could extend far beyond the initial sale.

Opportunities Beyond the Sale:

A million-dollar listing is not just about the immediate financial gain. It offers a multitude of opportunities that can significantly impact a broker's career. Working with HNWIs often involves managing their entire real estate portfolio, including acquisitions, sales, and property management. This comprehensive approach allows brokers to become indispensable advisors, guiding clients through complex transactions and helping them achieve their investment goals.

Additionally, high-value transactions enhance a broker's reputation and visibility in the industry. Successful sales of luxury properties often attract media attention and industry recognition, further establishing credibility and attracting new clients. This increased visibility can lead to invitations to exclusive industry events, collaborations with other top brokers, and access to premium listings.

LESSONS IN HUMAN BEHAVIOR:

One of the most valuable lessons I learned from selling million-dollar listings was understanding human behavior, particularly that of HNWIs. These clients are often driven by a desire for exclusivity, status, and convenience. They appreciate brokers who can provide personalized service, anticipate their needs, and deliver results efficiently.

For instance, during a high-stakes negotiation for a luxury property, I noticed that the client valued privacy and discretion above all else. To accommodate this, I arranged private viewings and ensured that all communications were confidential. By respecting his preferences and tailoring my approach accordingly, I was able to secure the deal and gain his trust.

Another important aspect of working with HNWIs is the ability to handle pressure and think quickly. These clients often have demanding schedules and expect prompt responses. I recall a situation where a client needed to finalize a purchase within a tight timeframe due to an impending overseas trip. By coordinating with all parties involved, expediting paperwork, and maintaining constant communication, I was able to close the deal in record time, much to the client's satisfaction.

The Value of Efficiency:

Efficiency is a key factor in successfully working with HNWIs. These clients value their time and expect seamless transactions. To meet these expectations, I developed a streamlined process that minimized delays and ensured smooth operations. This involved coordinating with lawyers, bankers, and other professionals to expedite procedures and provide clients with a hassle-free experience.

One example was a high-profile client who needed to sell his property quickly due to relocation. By leveraging my network and utilizing advanced marketing strategies, I was able to attract potential buyers swiftly and negotiate a favorable deal within the desired timeframe. This efficient approach not only earned the client's gratitude but also solidified my reputation as a reliable broker capable of handling urgent requests.

The Ripple Effect:

Securing a million-dollar listing can create a ripple effect of opportunities. Satisfied clients often refer their peers, leading to a network of high-net-worth individuals seeking similar services. This referral network can significantly expand a broker's client base and open doors to more lucrative transactions.

For instance, after successfully closing a deal for a luxury penthouse, the client referred me to a friend who was looking for a vacation home in an exclusive location. This referral led to another successful transaction, further establishing my presence in the luxury real estate market. Each successful deal built upon the previous one, creating a cycle of continuous growth and opportunities.

Conclusion:

Achieving a million-dollar listing was a pivotal moment in my career. It taught me invaluable lessons about human behavior, trust, efficiency, and the importance of thinking on my feet. Working with high-net-worth individuals provided opportunities beyond the immediate sale, including long-term relationships, referrals, and increased visibility in the industry.

By understanding the unique needs and preferences of HNWIs, delivering personalized service, and maintaining efficiency, I was able to build a reputation as a trusted broker capable of handling high-value transactions. The journey from small sales to million-dollar listings was challenging, but it paved the way for continued success and growth in the competitive world of real estate.

Chapter 6 emphasizes the significance of securing a million-dollar listing and the myriad opportunities it brings. Working with high-net-worth individuals requires understanding their unique behavior, building trust, and maintaining efficiency. By providing personalized service and thinking on your feet, you can establish long-term relationships, gain referrals, and enhance your reputation. Achieving a million-dollar listing is not just about immediate financial gain; it's about creating a ripple effect of opportunities that can significantly impact your career. This chapter underscores the importance of aiming high, staying adaptable, and delivering exceptional service to succeed in the luxury real estate market.

Chapter 7: Network Like a Pro.

Introduction:
Networking is the lifeblood of real estate. It's what transforms a good agent into a great one, what turns a single deal into a lifetime of opportunities. In this chapter, we'll dive into the art and science of networking, exploring the techniques and strategies that have propelled me to the top of the real estate world. Drawing inspiration from my personal experiences. this chapter will equip you with the tools to build a powerful network.

THE FOUNDATION OF NETWORKING:

Networking in real estate isn't just about collecting business cards or adding connections on LinkedIn; it's about building genuine, meaningful relationships. When I first started, I quickly realized that every interaction, no matter how small, could be an opportunity to strengthen my network. From the barista who made my coffee to the CEO of a major corporation, everyone became a potential ally or client.

RESPECT AND ATTENTION:

One of the earliest lessons I learned was the power of giving respect and attention. People love to feel important and heard. When you're in a conversation, be present. Listen actively, show genuine interest, and respect their opinions. This approach not only builds rapport but also fosters trust.

I remember an early client, Mrs. Thompson, who was selling her family home after her husband's passing. During our meetings, I didn't just focus on the sale; I listened to her stories about the house, her late husband, and the memories they shared. By giving her my full attention and respect, I built a connection that went beyond a mere transaction. She referred several clients to me, emphasizing how I made her feel valued during a difficult time.

Making Clients Feel Important:

In real estate, we're in the service business. Our clients' needs and issues must be our top priority. By resolving their concerns promptly and efficiently, we show them that they are important to us. This goes a long way in building loyalty and trust.

One particularly challenging client, Mr. Patel, was notorious for his high expectations and constant demands. Instead of being frustrated, I made it my

***

MISSION TO ADDRESS his concerns immediately. Whether it was a late-night call about a minor issue or a last-minute change in plans, I ensured he felt prioritized. Over time, this diligence paid off. Mr. Patel became one of my most loyal clients, referring numerous high-profile clients to me.

Playing Characters and Managing Personalities:

In real estate, you don't have a boss overseeing your interactions. You deal with a variety of clients, each with unique needs, attitudes, and personalities. Adapting to these different characters is crucial. Short-term ego control is often necessary to secure long-term success.

I had a client, Mr. Green, a high-powered executive with a massive ego. He was used to getting his way and didn't appreciate being contradicted. Instead of challenging him directly, I used subtle persuasion and flattery. I made him feel like every decision was his idea, even when guiding him toward the best choices. This approach, allowed me to close multiple high-value deals with him.

Setting Boundaries for Mutual Respect:

While accommodating clients is important, it's equally crucial to set boundaries. Mutual respect is the foundation of any successful relationship. Knowing when to stand firm is as important as knowing when to bend.

A particular instance stands out with a client, Ms. Rodriguez, who constantly overstepped boundaries, calling at odd hours and making unreasonable demands. I realized the need to establish clear boundaries while maintaining the relationship. I gently but firmly communicated my availability and set expectations. Surprisingly, this approach earned her respect, and our professional relationship improved significantly.

Building a Charismatic Rapport:

Charisma plays a vital role in networking. It's not just about being likable but about making people feel valued and understood. Whether through a warm smile, a firm handshake, or an engaging conversation, building a charismatic rapport can open doors that would otherwise remain closed.

Personal Tricks and Strategies:

1. Active Listening: Pay attention to what people say, respond thoughtfully, and show genuine interest. This makes people feel valued.

2. Personal Touch: Remember details about people's lives and bring them up in conversations. It shows you care beyond the business.

3. Follow-Up: Always follow up after meetings or transactions. A simple thank you note or a call can leave a lasting impression.

4. Be Genuine: Authenticity builds trust. Be yourself, and don't try to be someone you're not.

5. Adaptability: Be flexible in your approach. Understand the personality and needs of each client and adapt accordingly.

Networking Events and Social Gatherings:

Attending networking events and social gatherings is essential. These are prime opportunities to meet potential clients and industry professionals. Approach these events with a strategy. Set goals, know who you want to meet, and prepare talking points.

***

CASE STUDY: THE HIGH-Stakes Deal:

Let me share a story that encapsulates the power of networking in real estate. I was working on a high-stakes deal involving a luxury penthouse. The client, Mr. Anderson, was a high-profile businessman with a reputation for being difficult. My initial meetings with him were challenging; he was demanding and hard to please.

I spent time understanding his motivations and fears. I discovered he valued exclusivity and was driven by status. I tailored my approach, emphasizing the penthouse's unique features and its status symbol potential. I also leveraged my network to arrange a private tour of similar properties, showing him the exclusivity he craved.

Throughout the process, I made him feel important and respected. I addressed his concerns promptly and ensured he felt heard. I also set boundaries when needed, maintaining mutual respect. The deal closed successfully, and Mr. Anderson not only became a loyal client but also referred other high-profile clients to me.

Conclusion:

Networking is more than a business strategy; it's a way of life in real estate. Building genuine relationships, showing respect, managing personalities, and setting boundaries are essential skills. incorporating personal experiences, can transform your approach to networking. Remember, in real estate, your network is your net worth.

SUMMARY:

NETWORKING IN REAL estate is about building genuine relationships and giving respect and attention. Make clients feel important by prioritizing their needs and resolving issues promptly. Manage different personalities with tact and set boundaries for mutual respect. Use principles from "The Art of War" and "48 Laws of Power" to enhance your networking strategy. A strong network can propel your career to new heights.

Chapter 8: The Secret Sauce.

So, I realized that my secret sauce for getting ahead in my game totally depends on taking action, making myself and my skills better every single damn day. There was no chance, nor did I ever entertain giving clues or sharing my next step. I always think it as a jinx for the process. Sounds like someone you know, right?

When you're starting, it's crucial to understand what ideas, information, and actions to take. Early on, when you're figuring it out on your own, you don't have to be loud about it until...yes, until you've built a strong base for your actions. You must be prepared for any consequences because there's always resistance when you start something. The first step is taking action and then never giving up on yourself and your idea, no matter how many times you fail or how embarrassing it gets. Make consistency and discipline your primary habits.

Let's dive into a moment from my life where I thought of giving up. Yes, you heard it right. I feel so naive about it now that I was willing to give up everything for singing. Can you believe that I was willing to walk away from every good thing I had for singing? But now, see how the table turns out. This story is not about me making a vague decision; this is only one of the stories out of a thousand others. Case in point: it became my habit to be stubborn to get what I want. I got crazy about the things I wanted to do with my life, but this habit, when combined with my risk assessment skills, good decisions, a few mentors, and taking steps for action, started to work out. It led me to where I am today and will lead me to even greater heights.

THE EARLY REALIZATION:

In high school, I was always the kid who wanted more out of life. I had big dreams but wasn't entirely sure how to achieve them. I tried my hand at various hobbies, sports, and extracurricular activities, but nothing seemed to stick—until I discovered my passion for real estate. But before that, there was a time I nearly gave it all up for a different dream: singing.

The High School Blunder:

It was my sophomore year. I had just discovered my love for music, specifically singing. I wasn't particularly good at it, but I loved the idea of being on stage, performing in front of a crowd, and feeling the rush of adrenaline. One day, I decided to audition for the school talent show. I spent weeks practicing in front of the mirror, belting out tunes in my shower, and annoying my family with constant off-key renditions of pop songs.

The day of the audition arrived, and I was a bundle of nerves. I walked onto the stage, the bright lights blinding me momentarily. I took a deep breath and began to sing. To say it was a disaster would be an understatement. My voice cracked, I forgot the lyrics halfway through, and I could see the pained expressions on the judges' faces. I left the stage humiliated and convinced that I would never set foot in front of an audience again.

A Turning Point:

That night, I sat in my room, contemplating my future. I was so ready to give up on everything and focus solely on singing, despite my obvious lack of talent. My mom, sensing my distress, sat down beside me. She didn't offer empty platitudes or tell me I was amazing. Instead, she said, you have a lot of potential. You just need to find the right path. Singing may not be it, but don't let one failure define you."

Her words stuck with me. I realized that while singing wasn't my forte, I had other talents that I hadn't yet explored. I decided to focus on what I was good at and work on improving myself every day.

Discovering Real Estate:

Fast forward to my college years. I was still trying to figure out my path, but I knew one thing for sure: I was determined to succeed. I took a part-time job at a local real estate agency, initially just to make some extra cash. But as I learned more about the industry, I found myself genuinely interested. The idea of helping people find their dream homes, the thrill of closing a deal, and the potential for financial success—all of it appealed to me.

I started to immerse myself in real estate. I read books, attended endless seminars, and shadowed experienced agents. I quickly realized that the key to success in this field wasn't just knowledge—it was action. Every day, I set small goals for myself. I would make cold calls, visit properties, and network with potential clients. I learned to embrace rejection and use it as a learning opportunity.

Building the Habit of Action:

One of the most important lessons I learned was the power of consistency and discipline. It wasn't enough to work hard for a few days and then slack off. I had to be relentless in my pursuit of improvement. I made it a habit to review my goals every morning and take steps toward achieving them.

There were days when I felt like giving up. Rejection after rejection, deal after deal falling through—it was tough. But I reminded myself of my mom's words and the humiliation I felt on that stage. I wasn't going to let failure define me. Instead, I used it as fuel to keep going.

THE SECRET SAUCE: TAKING Action

Over time, I developed my "secret sauce" for success: taking action. It sounds simple, but it's incredibly powerful. Every day, I focused on getting better, even if it was just by a small margin. I didn't wait for the perfect moment or the right opportunity—I created my own opportunities.

I also learned the importance of keeping my plans to myself until they were ready to be executed. There's something about sharing your goals too early that can jinx the process. I became a firm believer in working quietly and letting my results speak for themselves.

MENTORSHIP AND GUIDANCE:

Another crucial element of my success was seeking mentorship. I was fortunate to find a few seasoned agents who were willing to take me under their wing. They taught me the ins and outs of the industry, shared their own mistakes and successes, and offered invaluable advice.

One mentor, in particular, stood out. He was a grizzled veteran of the real estate world, known for his no-nonsense approach and uncanny ability to close deals. He once told me, " in this business, you have to be like a shark. Always moving forward, never looking back. If you stop, even for a moment, you'll sink."

His words resonated with me. I realized that I needed to keep pushing forward, no matter what. I adopted his mentality and combined it with my own stubborn determination.

Blending Risk Assessment and Action:

As I gained more experience, I also became better at assessing risks. Real estate is a high-stakes game, and every decision carries potential consequences. I learned to weigh the pros and cons, analyze market trends, and make informed choices. But even with thorough risk assessment, there were no guarantees. That's where taking action came in.

I had to be willing to take calculated risks and accept the outcomes, good or bad.

One memorable experience was when I decided to invest in a property that many considered a lost cause. It was a run-down building in a less-than-desirable neighborhood. But I saw potential. I did my homework, ran the numbers, and took the plunge. It was a significant risk, but I was confident in my assessment.

The renovation process was grueling. There were setbacks, unexpected costs, and moments when I doubted my decision. But I stuck with it, taking action every day to move the project forward. In the end, my gamble paid off. The property turned out to be a lucrative investment, and it boosted my reputation in the industry.

The Humorous Side of Hustle:

OF COURSE, MY JOURNEY wasn't all serious business. There were plenty of humorous moments along the way.

Like the time I accidentally locked myself out of a client's house during a showing and had to climb through a window to let myself back in. Or the time I mistook a client's pet iguana for a decorative statue and nearly jumped out of my skin when it moved.

These moments, while embarrassing at the time, taught me not to take myself too seriously. They also reminded me that humor can be a powerful tool in building relationships. Clients appreciated my ability to laugh at myself and handle situations with grace and good humor.

The Journey Continues:

Looking back, I'm grateful for the twists and turns of my journey. From that disastrous singing audition to my first big real estate deal, every experience shaped me into the person I am today. My secret sauce—taking action, improving every day, and maintaining consistency and discipline—has been the foundation of my success.

I've learned that success isn't a destination but a continuous journey. There's always room for growth, new challenges to tackle, and higher heights to reach. And as I move forward, I carry with me the lessons of my past, the guidance of my mentors, and the unwavering belief in my ability to create my own path.

Summary:

The secret sauce to success lies in taking consistent action, improving your skills daily, and maintaining discipline. Early in your journey, focus on building a strong foundation and avoid sharing your plans too soon. Embrace failures as learning opportunities, seek mentorship, and blend risk assessment with decisive action. Remember to keep a sense of humor and stay resilient. Success is a continuous journey, and with the right mindset and habits, you can achieve great heights.

Chapter 9: Luxury, Sophistication, and Everything In Between.

Introduction:

When it comes to the world of real estate, luxury listings are not just about opulence and grandeur. They are a testament to professionalism, accountability, and the ability to handle immense pressure. This chapter delves into why I chose to specialize in luxury listings, the art of negotiating with high-net-worth individuals (HNWI), and the experiences that shaped my career. From my early days as an assistant to my transformation into a top-tier agent, this chapter is a journey through the intricate and sophisticated world of high-end real estate.

CHOOSING LUXURY LISTINGS: A Strategic Decision.

Choosing to focus on luxury listings wasn't merely a preference; it was a strategic decision. As a young agent, I quickly realized that luxury properties demanded a higher level of professionalism and accountability. With greater benefits come greater responsibilities. Handling these listings meant navigating complex deals, managing client expectations, and ensuring every detail was perfect. The pressure was immense, but it was also a driving force that pushed me to elevate my skills and standards.

VAN AMACE

My journey into the realm of luxury began during my time as an assistant to Adrian, an experienced multi-family agent. It was in this role that I discovered the intricacies of the market and the unique demands of HNWI clients. I learned that negotiating with millionaires was a different game altogether—they were like babies with machine guns, capable of pulling out of deals at any moment for personal reasons. This unpredictability required a blend of patience, finesse, and a deep understanding of their psyche.

THE ART OF FIGURING Out Your Talent:

One of the most valuable lessons I learned as Adrian's assistant was the importance of identifying and honing one's talent. In the bustling world of real estate, talent isn't just about selling properties; it's about understanding clients, anticipating their needs, and providing solutions that exceed their expectations. Working with Adrian, I was exposed to a myriad of scenarios that tested my abilities and pushed me to grow.

Adrian, a mentor with a no-nonsense approach, taught me the ropes of dealing with HNWI clients. His philosophy was simple: always be on your toes and never take a client's decision for granted. He emphasized the need for meticulous preparation and the ability to think on your feet. "These clients are straight shooters," he often said. "They can walk away from a deal just as quickly as they enter it. Your job is to ensure they stay."

Under Adrian's guidance, I developed a keen sense of market dynamics and honed my negotiation skills. I learned that dealing with millionaires required a unique blend of firmness and flexibility. They appreciated straightforwardness but also demanded a level of service that went beyond the ordinary. This experience was instrumental in shaping my approach to real estate and instilling in me a relentless drive to learn and improve.

THE EVERYTHING IN BETWEEN:

The path to success in luxury real estate is paved with countless experiences that shape one's skills and character. As an eager assistant, I immersed myself in every aspect of the business. I asked Adrian for as many tasks as possible, eager to be a crucial part of every deal. This proactive approach not only equipped me with practical knowledge but also helped me forge personal connections that would prove invaluable later in my career.

I remember one particular deal that tested my resilience and resourcefulness. A high-profile client was on the verge of closing a multi-million-dollar property when a last-minute issue threatened to derail the deal. Adrian was out of town, and the responsibility fell on my shoulders. I spent hours on the phone, coordinating with lawyers, financial advisors, and the client himself. My determination to see the deal through paid off, and we closed successfully. This experience taught me the importance of being prepared for any eventuality and reinforced my belief in the value of going the extra mile.

THE POWER OF PERSONALITY and Presentation:

While skills and knowledge are crucial, the true essence of success in luxury real estate lies in one's personality and presentation. My confidence and professionalism, particularly after college, played a significant role in my growth. One incident, in particular, stands out as a testament to the impact of personal presentation, of which my inspiration so much so inspired by "Harvey specter" and "James Bond" they really play a huge role for inspiring me for the style and taste in clothes I have now.

I was meeting a new client, a discerning individual known for his attention to detail. As I arrived in my best three-piece suit, I could see the client appraising me from head to toe. The way I greeted him, addressed his concerns, and presented myself left a lasting impression. He later confided that my appearance and demeanor had instilled confidence in him. "You look like someone who knows his business," he said. This encounter underscored the importance of dressing well and presenting oneself with confidence and poise.

Another memorable story involved a high-net-worth client who had a penchant for meticulous detail. He was hesitant about a particular property due to a minor issue with the landscaping. While many agents might have dismissed his concern, I saw it as an opportunity to go above and beyond. I personally oversaw the landscaping adjustments, ensuring everything was to his satisfaction. The client was not only impressed but also became a loyal advocate, referring several high-profile clients to me.

These experiences reinforced the significance of the "everything in between"—the small, often overlooked aspects that contribute to building trust and making a lasting impression. It wasn't just about closing deals; it was about creating memorable experiences for clients and demonstrating a genuine commitment to their satisfaction.

HUMOR AND HUMILITY in High-Stakes Situations:

Navigating the world of luxury real estate often involved high-stakes situations that required a blend of humor and humility. One particularly challenging deal involved a client with an eccentric sense of humor. He enjoyed testing agents with outlandish requests and quirky comments. While some agents found him exasperating, I saw an opportunity to connect on a personal level.

During one of our meetings, he jokingly mentioned wanting a hidden room in his new property, reminiscent of a spy movie. Rather than dismissing his comment, I played along, suggesting creative ideas for secret doors and hidden passages. This lighthearted approach not only entertained him but also built a rapport that facilitated smoother negotiations. The deal closed successfully, and the client appreciated my willingness to engage with his unique personality.

Humor also played a crucial role in diffusing tense situations. In another instance, a deal was on the brink of collapse due to a miscommunication between the buyer and seller. Tensions were high, and tempers flared. Sensing the need for a break, I suggested we all take a moment to share a funny story or joke. The simple act of laughing together eased the tension, allowing us to resume negotiations with a clearer, calmer mindset. The deal was saved, and both parties left satisfied.

These experiences taught me the value of humor and humility in high-pressure situations. They reminded me that even in the most serious of professions, a light-hearted approach could foster stronger relationships and lead to better outcomes.

Reflections and Lessons Learned:

As I reflect on my journey in luxury real estate, several key lessons stand out. First and foremost is the importance of continuous learning. Every deal, every client, and every challenge presented an opportunity to grow and refine my skills. Embracing this mindset allowed me to stay ahead in a competitive market and consistently deliver exceptional results.

Another crucial lesson was the significance of building genuine relationships. High-net-worth clients valued trust and reliability above all else. By prioritizing their needs, going the extra mile, and maintaining a personal touch, I was able to establish long-lasting connections that went beyond mere transactions.

Lastly, the power of presentation and personality cannot be overstated. In a field where first impressions matter immensely, dressing well, exuding confidence, and treating clients with utmost respect made all the difference. These elements, combined with a relentless drive for excellence, formed the foundation of my success in luxury real estate.

Conclusion.

"Luxury, Sophistication, and Everything In Between" is not just a chapter title; it's a reflection of the journey, the challenges, and the triumphs that have defined my career. From the early days of figuring out my talent to mastering the art of dealing with high-net-worth clients, every experience has contributed to my growth. This chapter encapsulates the essence of what it means to thrive in the world of luxury real estate—a blend of professionalism, resilience, humor, and an unwavering commitment to excellence.

SUMMARY.

This chapter delves into the strategic decision to specialize in luxury listings, emphasizing the need for professionalism and accountability. It highlights the importance of identifying and honing one's talent, particularly in dealing with high-net-worth individuals. Through personal anecdotes, it showcases the significance of presentation and personality in making a lasting impression. The chapter also underscores the value of humor and humility in high-stakes situations, illustrating how these traits can foster stronger relationships and better outcomes. Ultimately, it reflects on the lessons learned and the journey of continuous growth and excellence in the field of luxury real estate.

# Chapter 10: When the Going Gets Tough.

Real estate is not for the faint-hearted. It's a rollercoaster ride with exhilarating highs and crushing lows. Statistics show that around 60% of real estate agents drop out within their first year. This isn't just a fleeting trend—it fluctuates with the economy, inflation, interest rates, and various other factors. However, some agents persist and thrive regardless of market conditions. They aren't supernaturally gifted; they're productive, resilient, and possess a remarkable level of patience. This chapter delves into what separates those who thrive from those who don't, with a special focus on an unforgettable client encounter with Mr. Powell.

UNDERSTANDING THE MARKET Dynamics:

The real estate market is unpredictable. Economic shifts, policy changes, and market trends can drastically affect the industry. During my early years, I faced several economic downturns that tested my resolve. It was during these tough times that I learned a crucial lesson: "Follow up, follow up, follow up." This mantra became my guiding light.

In luxury real estate, patience is not just a virtue; it's a necessity. High-end clients have unique needs and preferences, and the buying process can be lengthy and demanding. Sometimes, after months of showing properties, clients might walk away due to minor details or opt to work with another agent, often due to family connections. It's easy to feel defeated, but this is where resilience and patience come into play.

THE STORY OF MR. POWELL:

I remember a particularly challenging client, Mr. Powell. He was a high-profile businessman with an eye for detail and an uncompromising attitude. Our journey together taught me invaluable lessons about patience, perseverance, and the art of follow-up.

Mr. Powell had a reputation for being meticulous. He'd been through several agents and was known for his exacting standards. When he approached me, I knew I was in for a test. Our first meeting was in my office, where he laid out his expectations with military precision. He wanted a property that was nothing short of perfect.

THE SEARCH BEGINS:

We began our search with enthusiasm. The first few properties we visited were stunning, each offering something unique. However, Mr. Powell always found something amiss. The kitchen island was too small, the master bedroom lacked natural light, or the backyard didn't have the right view. Each rejection chipped away at my confidence, but I kept reminding myself of the importance of persistence.

Our property tours were exhaustive. We visited over fifty homes, each one meticulously analyzed and critiqued. There were times when I thought he was intentionally finding faults to test me. But every time he rejected a property, I took it as a learning opportunity. I refined my understanding of his preferences, noting every detail he mentioned.

THE TURNING POINT:

After months of searching, I found a property that seemed to tick all the boxes. It was a luxurious mansion with expansive views, state-of-the-art amenities, and a prime location. I was excited, confident that this would finally be the one. Mr. Powell walked through the house, his expression unreadable. After an hour of thorough inspection, he turned to me and said, "It's nice, but it's not for me."

I was crestfallen. This was the closest we had come to finding his dream home, and yet, it wasn't enough. I thanked him for his time and promised to keep looking. As I walked away, I felt a pang of self-doubt. Was I not good enough? Was there something I was missing?

A LESSON IN PATIENCE:

Months passed, and the property search continued. I was determined not to give up. One evening, while reviewing new listings, I received a call from Mr. Powell. He sounded unusually relaxed. "Can we meet tomorrow?" he asked. I agreed, curious about the sudden change in tone.

THE NEXT DAY, WE MET at a coffee shop. To my surprise, Mr. Powell wasn't there to discuss a new property. Instead, he wanted to talk about the process. He confessed that he appreciated my persistence and dedication. "You've shown me properties tirelessly, always with a smile and a positive attitude. I've worked with many agents, but none have been as patient and attentive as you."

THE PAYOFF.

Mr. Powell's words were a turning point. It wasn't just about finding the perfect property; it was about building trust and demonstrating commitment. Shortly after our conversation, I found another property. It was a stunning estate with all the features Mr. Powell desired. This time, he was impressed. We made an offer, and within a few weeks, the deal was closed.

REFLECTIONS ON RESILIENCE:

The experience with Mr. Powell was a testament to the power of patience and perseverance. It reinforced the importance of follow-up and the need to stay positive even when the going gets tough. Many agents give up after a few setbacks, but those who persist are the ones who succeed.

THE BROADER LESSON:

In real estate, you'll face clients who test your patience and resilience. They might look at hundreds of houses, nitpick over minor details, or ultimately choose another agent. It's crucial to remember that this is part of the process. The luxury market, in particular, is about providing the best possible service and making lasting connections. Even if a client doesn't choose you initially, your dedication and professionalism will leave a lasting impression.

Over time, I've learned not to compare myself to others. Instead, I focus on what I can control: my work ethic, my attitude, and my service quality. I've had clients who initially bought with someone else but later returned to me because they recognized the value of my individualized, exclusive services. The key is to keep improving, stay patient, and always give your best.

CONCLUSION.

When the going gets tough, it's the resilient, patient, and persistent agents who rise to the top. The journey with Mr. Powell was challenging, but it taught me invaluable lessons that shaped my career. Real estate is not just about making sales; it's about building relationships, earning trust, and providing exceptional service.

Summary:

This chapter underscores the importance of patience, perseverance, and resilience in real estate. Through the story of Mr. Powell, it highlights the challenges of dealing with meticulous clients and the value of follow-up and dedication. Success in real estate is about more than just closing deals; it's about building lasting relationships and providing unparalleled service.

Chapter 11: Sales & Closing.

In real estate, or any sales job, one thing many people fail to differentiate is the distinction between making a sale and closing a deal. Whether you're selling cars, real estate, or any product or service, you've probably noticed that some people can call thousands of leads, work tirelessly, and yet their sales figures barely move. On the other hand, there's the individual who seems to close every deal they touch. What sets them apart? In previous chapters, we've touched on some crucial points: if you want to temper or destroy your sales, show your desperation. Now, let's delve deeper into the unique skill sets that differentiate a closer from a mere salesperson: patience, understanding the client's needs, and the charm that infuses confidence in their product.

THE ROOKIE STRUGGLE:

In my early days as a rookie real estate agent, I was all hustle and no finesse. I would wake up early, dress sharply, and spend my days cold calling potential leads, attending networking events, and arranging viewings. I believed that sheer effort would be enough to propel me to the top. But reality had other plans.

I remember one listing in particular—a charming two-bedroom house in a decent neighborhood. It wasn't luxurious, but it had potential. I poured my heart into marketing it. Flyers, online listings, open houses—you name it, I did it. Despite my efforts, weeks went by without a single offer. I began to question my skills and felt a creeping sense of desperation.

Then came the open house that shattered my confidence. Another agent, Mark, had a similar listing just a few blocks away. While I was struggling to get a handful of visitors to my open house, his was packed. By the end of the week, he had closed the deal. I was devastated.

LEARNING FROM THE BEST:

Determined to understand what I was doing wrong, I swallowed my pride and approached Mark. I remember feeling a mix of embarrassment and curiosity as I asked him, "What did you do differently? How did you sell that house so quickly?"

Mark looked at me, surprised by my candid admission of defeat. After a moment, he smirked and said, "Come, let's grab a coffee."

Over coffee, Mark didn't give me a magic formula. Instead, he shared his approach. " selling is one thing, but closing—that's an art. It's not just about showing the house. It's about making the buyer feel something. You have to connect with them, understand their needs, and then make them see how this house can fulfill those needs."

He talked about the importance of patience. "You can't rush a buyer. Desperation kills deals. You have to be patient, listen to their concerns, and address them genuinely."

Then he emphasized understanding the client. "Every buyer is different. Some are looking for a home, others an investment. You have to tailor your approach based on what they're looking for."

Finally, he touched on the charm and confidence. "You have to believe in what you're selling. Your enthusiasm is contagious. If you're excited about the house, the buyer will be too."

PUTTING LESSONS INTO Practice:

Armed with this new perspective, I decided to test Mark's advice. My next listing was a small but cozy apartment. Instead of just focusing on the features of the apartment, I tried to connect with each potential buyer. I asked about their lifestyle, their needs, and their dreams.

One couple, in particular, stood out. They were newlyweds looking for their first home. Instead of just showing them the apartment, I painted a picture of their future. "Imagine coming home after a long day and relaxing in this cozy living room. The kitchen is perfect for the dinner parties you mentioned you love hosting. And the bedroom—imagine waking up here every morning."

I watched their faces light up as they envisioned their life in the apartment. My enthusiasm and confidence were infectious. By the end of the week, they made an offer.

THE DIFFERENCE BETWEEN Sales and Closing:

From that moment, I understood the crucial difference between sales and closing. A property can attract a buyer, but what sells the house is the energy, enthusiasm, and emotions you trigger in them. It's about making them see not just a house, but a home.

As my career progressed, I honed these skills further. I learned that every client interaction was an opportunity to build a connection. I started to enjoy the process of understanding each client's unique needs and tailoring my approach to meet them.

THE ART OF CLOSING.

The art of closing deals is about more than just finalizing a transaction. It's about creating a sense of urgency without desperation. It's about making the buyer feel valued and understood. Here are some key takeaways that have helped me close deals successfully:

1. Build Rapport: Establish a connection with your clients. Make them feel comfortable and valued.

2. Listen Actively: Pay attention to their needs and concerns. Show genuine interest in understanding what they're looking for.

3. Address Concerns: Don't brush off their worries. Address them thoughtfully and provide solutions.

4. Create a Vision: Help them envision their life in the property. Paint a picture of the future that aligns with their dreams.

5. Exude Confidence: Believe in the value of what you're selling. Your confidence will instill confidence in the buyer.

6. Follow Up: Don't let leads go cold. Follow up regularly and show that you're committed to helping them find the perfect property.

FROM SALESMAN TO CLOSER:

My journey from a struggling salesman to a confident closer was filled with challenges and learning experiences. I learned that closing deals required a different set of skills than just selling. It required patience, understanding, and a genuine connection with the client.

One of my most memorable experiences was with a luxury penthouse listing. The potential buyer was a high-net-worth individual with very specific tastes. Instead of just showcasing the property, I took the time to understand his lifestyle and preferences. I learned that he loved art, so I highlighted the penthouse's potential as an art gallery. I knew he valued privacy, so I emphasized the secure, exclusive nature of the building.

During the viewing, I spoke with enthusiasm and confidence, painting a vivid picture of how the penthouse would complement his lifestyle. By the end of the tour, he was sold—not just on the property, but on the vision I had created for him.

CONCLUSION.

The difference between sales and closing is subtle but profound. It's about moving from a transactional mindset to a relational one. It's about understanding that while anyone can show a property, it takes a true closer to make a buyer see it as their future home.

As you navigate your own journey in sales, remember that the skills of closing can be learned and honed. Focus on building genuine connections, understanding your clients, and exuding confidence and enthusiasm. With these skills, you can turn every lead into a closed deal.

Summary:

CLOSING DEALS IN REAL estate involves more than just selling properties. It requires building rapport, listening actively, addressing concerns, creating a vision, exuding confidence, and following up. The difference between a salesperson and a closer lies in their ability to connect with clients and make them see the property as their future home. Through patience, understanding, and enthusiasm, you can transform your sales approach and achieve greater success.

PART -2,

To be continued....

Also by Van Amace

OWN IT WITH VANAMACE
OWN IT WITH VANAMACE>

www.ingramcontent.com/pod-product-compliance
Lightning Source LLC
Chambersburg PA
CBHW031738150726
47989CB00006B/2510